## DATE DUE

|  |  |  |  |
|---|---|---|---|
|  |  |  |  |
|  |  |  |  |
|  |  |  |  |
|  |  |  |  |
|  |  |  |  |
|  |  |  |  |
|  |  |  |  |
|  |  |  |  |
|  |  |  |  |
|  |  |  |  |
|  |  |  |  |
|  |  |  |  |

## Dedication

To all the children who write me encouraging letters about my books, with much appreciation for their thoughtfulness.

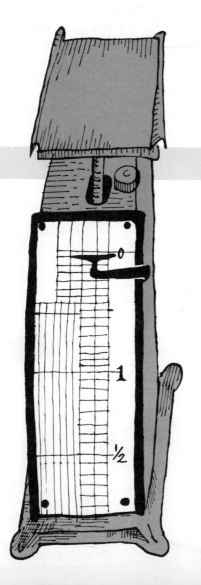

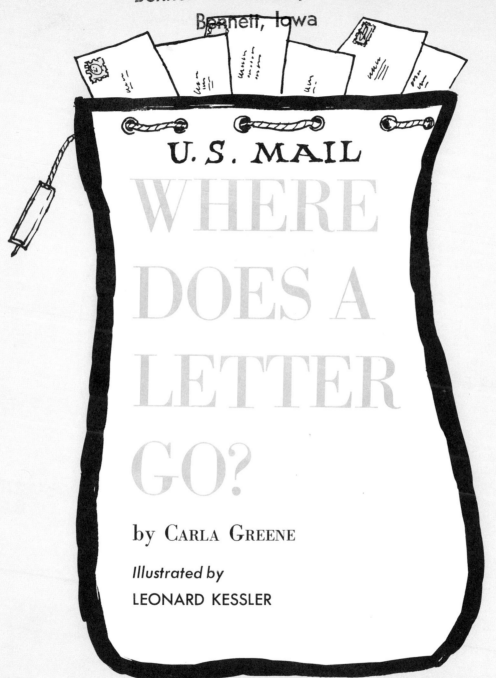

U.S. MAIL

# WHERE DOES A LETTER GO?

by CARLA GREENE

*Illustrated by*
LEONARD KESSLER

 HARVEY HOUSE, INC., *Publishers*
IRVINGTON-ON-HUDSON, NEW YORK

**HARVEY HOUSE, INC.,** *Publishers*
IRVINGTON-ON-HUDSON, NEW YORK

Text © 1966 by Carla Greene
Illustrations © 1966 by Harvey House, Inc.

Library of Congress Catalog Card Number: 65-24968
Manufactured in the United States of America

# CONTENTS

## Acknowledgment

The author wishes to thank personnel of the UNITED STATES POST OFFICE for reading this manuscript and making helpful suggestions as well as approving contents for accuracy.

### Danny Makes a Wish

"I wish Cousin Jane would come to visit me," said Danny to his mother one morning.

"Wishing is fine," said Mother. "But Jane is far away. If you want your wish to come true, it is better to write her a letter and ask her to visit you."

Mother was right. If Danny wrote his wish in a letter, perhaps the wish would come true.

# You Can Send a Letter Anywhere

You can send a letter to an Eskimo in Alaska.
You can send a letter to a lion hunter in Africa.

You can send a letter to a snake charmer in India.

You can send a letter to a pearl diver in Japan.

You can send a letter anywhere. Anywhere in the whole world.

11

# Letters of Long Ago

Long, long ago, only a king or a very rich man could send a letter.

He wrote his letter on the skin of a sheep or a goat.

He rolled it up.

And he gave the letter to his slave to carry.

The slave ran and ran and ran. He ran for miles and miles.

It took a long time to deliver a letter. It took months, and sometimes even years.

## The Pony Express

When our country was new, letters were sent by riders on horses.

This way of sending our mail was called the PONY EXPRESS.

The horses ran fast, fast, fast! But horses get tired. And riders get tired too.

When the rider got tired he stopped and gave his bag of letters to another rider.

The second rider started out on another horse.

The horse ran many miles.

Then the second rider stopped and gave the bag of letters to a third rider.

The horse ran fast. But it still took weeks or months to deliver a letter.

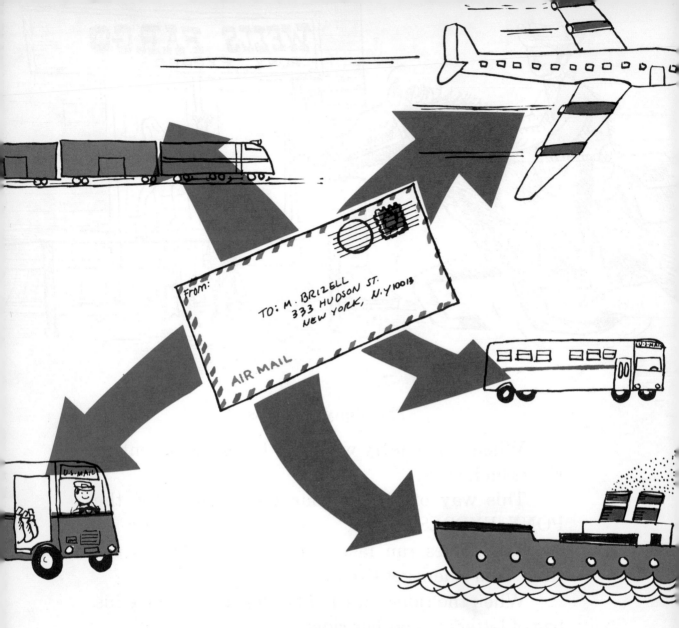

### Sending a Letter Now

Now you can send a letter in a short time.

It costs only a few pennies.

Your letter may go on a train, a bus, a truck, or a ship.

If you want your letter to go extra fast, you can send it on an airplane. This is called AIR MAIL.

14

## Danny Writes a Letter

That afternoon, Danny wrote a letter to Jane. The letter said:

Dear Jane:

I wish you would come to visit me. You can come on a train, or a bus, or a plane. But please come soon.

Danny

Danny put the letter into an envelope. He wrote Jane's name and address on it. He also wrote his own name and address in the upper left hand corner of the envelope.

Danny showed the envelope to his mother.

"Did you forget something?" asked Mother.

"I don't think so," said Danny.

"Yes, you did," said Mother. "You forgot to put the ZIP CODE number after the city and state. The ZIP CODE helps the postmen to sort the letters and to deliver them faster."

Danny wrote the ZIP CODE number right after the city and state of Jane's address. He also wrote the ZIP CODE number after his own address in the upper left hand corner of the envelope.

The envelope looked like this:

Danny Jones
820 Fairmont Ave.
Los Angeles, Cal. 90005

Jane Brown
5200 Shore Road
Fremont, Maine 04032

"Your letter will reach Jane faster if you send it by AIR MAIL," said Mother. "Just write AIR MAIL on the envelope and we will take it to the post office and mail it."

"Can't I mail the letter in the box at the corner?" asked Danny. "I have seen the postman come in his mail truck and take letters out of the box. He told me he takes the letters to the post office."

"We do not have an AIR MAIL stamp, so we had better go to the post office and buy one. Besides, your letter will go faster if you mail it at the post office," said Mother.

Danny's mother went on, "I have some shopping to do, so I can take you to the main post office downtown. Your letter will go off even faster from there."

Danny wanted his letter to go fast. So he and his mother took his letter to the big main post office.

## At the Post Office

Danny saw many interesting things at the post office.

He saw rows and rows of little boxes—one little box after the other. Each little box had a window in it, so you could see if there was any mail in the box.

A man opened one of the little boxes with a key. He took out some letters. The man rents this box from the post office. He comes here and gets his mail instead of having the postman bring it to him.

Also some people who have business firms have their mail sent to a post office box. This way, they can have a business address without having a store or office.

Danny saw a counter marked PARCEL POST. People holding packages stood in line.

The clerk behind the desk took a woman's package. He looked at the address. Then he weighed the package.

"This will cost forty cents," said the clerk. The woman gave the clerk the money.

When you send a package by PARCEL POST, you pay for the number of miles it is going and for the number of pounds it weighs.

Suddenly Danny stopped and listened. CHEEP CHEEP—he heard. It sounded like baby chicks. But what were baby chicks doing in a post office.

Danny looked around. Sure enough, a man with a box of baby chicks was waiting in the PARCEL POST line. Baby chicks, ducks, and geese can be sent by PARCEL POST when they are one day old. They do not need food or water for the first sixty hours.

Danny saw a window with a sign over it reading GENERAL DELIVERY.

"What does it mean?" he asked Mother.

"When people move to a new city and are not sure of where they are going to live, they have their letters sent to the post office. They come to this window to get their letters," said Mother.

Over another window there was a sign that read REGISTRY. When you send money through the mail, you pay a little extra postage to have it registered. Then if the money should get lost, the post office will pay it back to you.

Danny went to the window marked STAMPS.
He bought an AIR MAIL stamp.
He licked the stamp and stuck it on the letter.
"Now where does the letter go?" asked Danny.
"Drop it into the slot marked AIR MAIL," said
his mother.

Danny saw three slots. The slots were marked:

CITY     OUT OF TOWN     AIR MAIL

Danny put his letter into the slot that was marked AIR MAIL.

The letter dropped into a sack which was on the other side of the wall.

"Now is my letter on its way to Jane?" asked Danny.

"Yes," said his mother. "And now let's go shopping."

### What Happens to Danny's Letter?

What happens to Danny's letter after it has dropped into the sack?

How will the letter get to Jane?

Would you like to know?

Come and see what goes on in the back of the post office in a large city.

## Behind the Scenes

Letters. Letters. Letters. Sacks and sacks full of letters.

The sacks are emptied onto long tables called batching tables.

Piles and piles of letters. Short envelopes. Long envelopes.

What will happen to all the letters now?

Jim and Tom are workers at the post office. They
are called clerks.

Jim and Tom and some other clerks stand at the
long batching tables. They put the letters into trays.

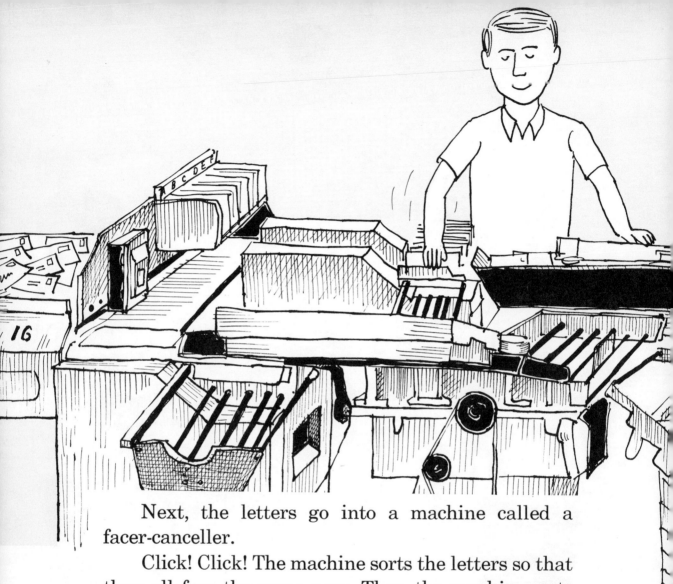

Next, the letters go into a machine called a facer-canceller.

Click! Click! The machine sorts the letters so that they all face the same way. Then the machine puts a black mark across the stamp. Now no one can use that stamp again.

The machine also prints on the envelope the name of the city and state, the date, and A. M. or P. M., to show what part of the day it is.

And the machine counts too. It counts each letter.

In smaller post offices, where they do not have a facer-canceller, the clerks sort the letters by hand. But a machine does the rest of the work.

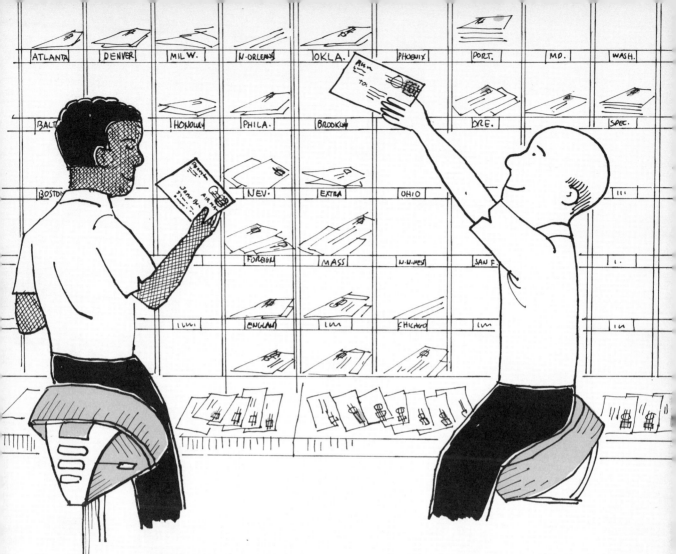

Now Jim and Tom sit in front of rows and rows of open boxes. On each box is the name of a large city or a state.

If a letter is going to a large city, it goes into the box that has the name of that city on it.

If a letter is going to a small city or town, it goes into the box that has the name of the *state* marked on it. These letters are sorted again into the towns where each is going and are tied into separate bundles.

Now all the letters for the same city or town are in the same bundle.

Sacks. Sacks. Sacks.

Each sack has a label with the name of a large city or a state on it. Into the sacks where each belongs, go the tied bundles of letters.

AIR MAIL letters are sorted by themselves and tied into bundles just as other letters are. But they are thrown into their own AIR MAIL sacks. The color of these sacks is bright orange, so it is easy to tell them apart from other sacks.

Many people send AIR MAIL letters in envelopes with red-white-and-blue stripes around them. This helps the clerks to see them quickly.

Danny's letter is in a plain white envelope, but it has AIR MAIL written on it, and it also has an AIR MAIL stamp, so it goes into an AIR MAIL orange-colored sack.

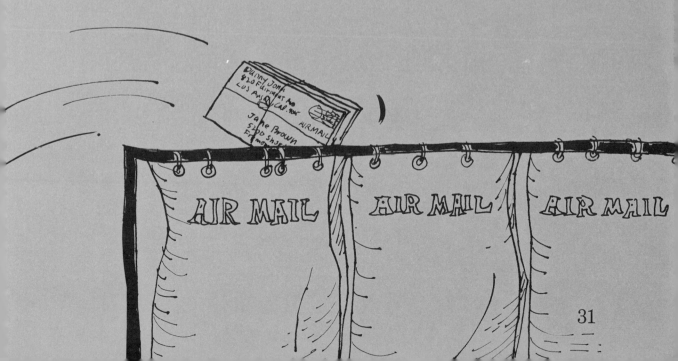

# Loading and Unloading Mail

Trucks. Trucks. Trucks.

They bring the letters that the postmen take out of the mail boxes all over the city.

Some mail trucks bring the letters that come from faraway places.

Some trucks pick up sacks of letters that are going out of the post office to places nearby and far away. Some trucks take AIR MAIL letters to the airport.

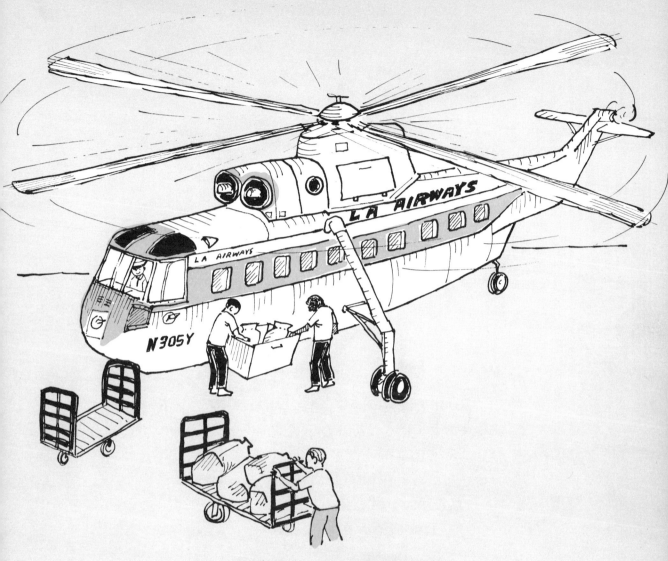

### Off Goes the Helicopter!

In some places, a helicopter takes AIR MAIL letters from a nearby heliport to the airport.

One, two, three — the helicopter lands at the heliport.

Into the helicopter go the sacks of AIR MAIL.

A few minutes later the helicopter lands at the airport.

### Danny's Letter Goes on an Airplane

At the airport, the sacks of mail are taken off the trucks and helicopters. They are loaded into smaller trucks that take them to the plane.

One part of the plane carries AIR MAIL. People ride in the other part of the plane.

There goes the sack with Danny's letter in it.

The sack rides up on a moving belt into the plane.

The plane flies fast, fast, fast!

Just a few hours go by. The plane lands at an airport. This airport is thousands of miles away from the place where the plane started.

Now Danny's letter is getting closer and closer to Jane.

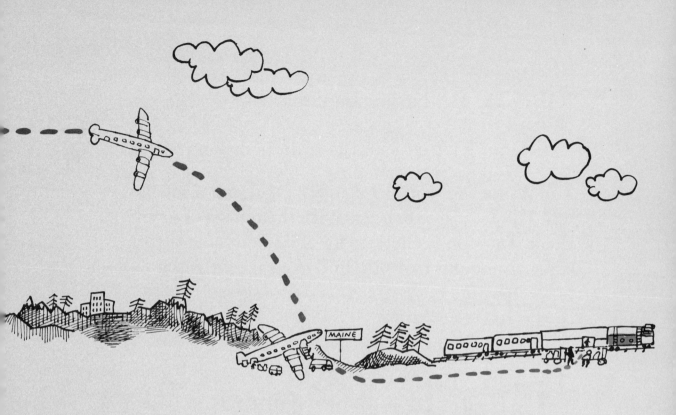

### From the Airplane to a Train

Jane lives in a town that is a hundred miles from the airport.

When letters addressed to Jane arrive at the airport, they must be put on a train that stops at Jane's town.

First, the letters are picked up by a mail truck. The truck brings sacks of letters from the airport to the nearest post office, where they are again sorted. Then another truck takes them to the train.

One of the cars on the train is called the RAILWAY MAIL car. Into this car go the sacks of mail.

Danny's letter is on the train in one of the sacks.

While the train runs, clerks sort the mail.

They sort it into boxes with the names of towns on them. They tie the letters for the same town together. They throw the tied pile into the sack with the name of the town on it.

The train stops at the railroad station in Jane's town. A sack of mail is tossed off the train.

A mail truck picks up the sack of mail.

Off to the town's post office goes the sack with Danny's letter in it.

In some places, mail goes on a bus called a HIGHWAY POST OFFICE. The inside of the bus is similar to the inside of the RAILWAY MAIL car. Clerks work on the bus just as they do on a train.

## The Postman Picks Up the Mail

Early in the morning, the postman walks up the steps of the post office in Jane's town.

He comes to pick up the mail that he will deliver to people today.

What does the postman do first?
You guessed it!
He sorts the mail.
He sorts it into little boxes.
He puts the letters in order so he can go from one house to the next.
The postman fills his bag or caddy-type cart with letters, papers, and magazines.
He leaves the mail he cannot carry or put into his cart.

A mail truck comes and picks up the mail that the postman cannot carry. The truck brings the extra mail to a storage box.

When the postman's bag or cart is empty, he goes to the storage box and opens it with a key. He fills his bag or cart with mail again.

The postman does not carry packages in his bag. The PARCEL POST truck picks up the packages at the post office. The driver of the truck is also a postman. He brings the packages to people's houses.

# The Country Postman

Some people live in the country.

The country postman brings the mail in an automobile.

He leaves the letters in a mailbox by the side of the road.

## A Letter for Jane

Jane lives in a middle-size town. The postman brings the mail right to Jane's house.

One day the postman said, "Here is a letter for you, Jane."

"Thank you, thank you!" cried Jane. "I like to get letters."

Jane read Danny's letter. It made her very happy.

"Danny wants me to come to visit him," cried Jane. "May I go? May I go?"

"Yes," said Jane's mother. "You may go in the summer."

### Danny's Wish Comes True

So one day in the summer, Jane went to visit her cousin Danny.

She went on a plane.

She flew as fast as an air mail letter.

Jane had a good time.

Danny had a good time too.

And it all happened because Danny wrote a letter to Jane.